101 Re
Not To Do Anything

A Collection of
Cynical & Defeatist
Quotations

Summersdale Publishers Ltd
46 West Street
Chichester
West Sussex
PO19 1RP UK

A CIP catalogue record for this book is available from the British Library.
Printed and bound in Great Britain

ISBN 1 84024 043 1

101 Reasons Not To Do Anything

A Collection of Cynical & Defeatist Quotations

Introduction

According to Oscar Wilde, a cynic is 'A man who knows the price of everything and the value of nothing', which is a refreshing antidote to the feel-good, be calm, de-stress and motivational trends that have crept into our society in recent years.

It wasn't always like this. In past centuries people would look at the world through grey-tinted spectacles. So what better way to combat the nicey nicey nineties than with this treasure trove of the world's finest cynical and defeatest quotations?

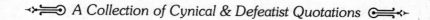

If you live long enough, you'll see that
every victory turns into a defeat.

Simone de Beavoir
Touts les hommes sont mortels

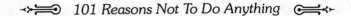

I want to be bored to death,
as good a way to go as any.

Peter De Vries
Comfort me with Apples

Other people are quite dreadful.
The only possible society is oneself.

Oscar Wilde
An Ideal Husband

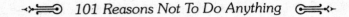

I get my exercise acting as a pall bearer
to my friends who exercise.

Chauncey Depew

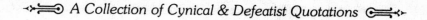

Happy is the man with a wife to tell him
what to do and a secretary to do it.

Lord Mancroft
Observer, "Sayings of the Week" 18 Dec 1966

Alas! The hours we waste in work
and similar inconsequence,
Friends, I beg you do not shirk
Your daily task of indolence.

Don Marquis
The Almost Perfect State

It is better to have loafed and lost
than never to have loafed at all.

James Thurber
Fables for Our Time, "The Courtship of All"

'Tis the voice of the sluggard, I hear him complain;
"You have waked me too soon, I must slumber again".

Isaac Watts
The Sluggard

I am happiest when I am idle. I could live for months without performing any kind of labour, and at the expiration of that time I should feel fresh and vigorous enough to go right on in the same time for numerous more months.

Artemus Ward
Pyrotechny

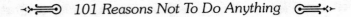

It was such a lovely day
I thought it was a pity to get up.

W. Somerset Maughan
Our Betters

I enjoy convalescence. It is the part that makes the illness worthwhile.

George Bernard Shaw
Back to Methuselah

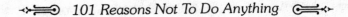

I am interested in leisure in the way a poor man is interested in money. I can't get enough of it.

Attributed to Prince Philip

The wisdom of a learned man cometh by opportunity of leisure: and he that hath little business shall become wise.

Bible
Ecclesiastes 38. 24-25

You should do nothing that did not absolutely please you. Be idle, be very idle! The habits of your mind are such that you will necessarily do much; but be as idle as you can.

S.T. Coleridge
Letter to Southey

Every man is, or hopes to be, an Idler

Samuel Johnson
The Idler

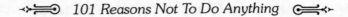

I am sure that indolence – indefeasible indolence –
is the true state of man, and business
the invention of the old Teazer.

Charles Lamb
Letter to Wordsworth, 1805

There is one piece of advice, in a life of study, which I think no one will object to; and that is, every now and then to be completely idle, – to do nothing at all.

Sydney Smith
Sketches of Moral Philosophy

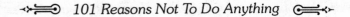

Increased means and increased leisure
are the two civilisers of men.

Benjamin Disraeli
Speech to Conservatives of Manchester, 3 April 1872

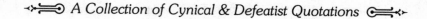

Leisure is the mother of Philosophy.

Thomas Hobbes
Leviathan *iv, 46*

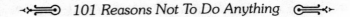

Leisure is the best of all possessions.

Socrates
Diogenes Laertius

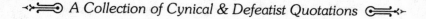

There is no pleasure in having nothing to do;
the fun is having lots to do and not doing it.

Mary Wilson Little

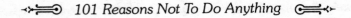

What's wrong with dropping out?
To me, this is the whole point: one's right
to withdraw from a social environment that
offers no spiritual sustenance, and to
mind one's own business.

William S Burroughs

One little chore to do, one little commission to fulfil,
one message to carry, would spoil heaven itself.

Henry D Thoreau
Journal, 21 July 1851

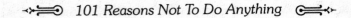

So that what was indolence was called wisdom.

Tacitus

I have spent my life laboriously doing nothing.

Grotius

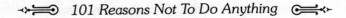

With ecstasies so sweet
As none can ever guess
Who walk not with the feet
Of joy in idleness

Robert Bridges
Spring

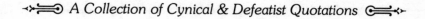

That indolent but delightful
condition of doing nothing.

Pliny the Younger

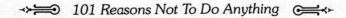

Better to idle well than work badly.

Spanish proverb

Serious matters can wait until tomorrow.

Cornelius Nepos
Pelopidas

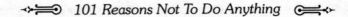

To do nothing is in every man's power.

Samuel Johnson
The Rambler

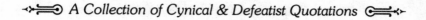

Procrastination
– the art of keeping up with yesterday.

Don Marquis

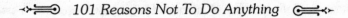

Never put off until tomorrow what you can
do the day after tomorrow just as well.

Mark Twain
The Late Benjamin Franklin

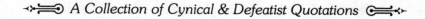

Work is the refuge of people who
have nothing better to do.

Oscar Wilde

. . . saves time like putting off until tomorrow
what you should do today.

Malcolm Muggeridge

My father taught me to work, but not to love it. I never did like to work, and I don't deny it. I'd rather read, tell stories, crack jokes, talk, laugh – anything but work.

Abraham Lincoln

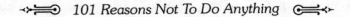

The chief attraction of military service has
consisted and will consist in this
compulsory and irreproachable idleness.

Tolstoy
War and Peace

Put off the evil hour as long as you can.

Proverb

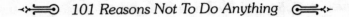

As peace is the end of war, so to be idle is
the ultimate purpose of the busy.

Samuel Johnson
The Idler

He that knows nothing, doubts nothing.

Proverb

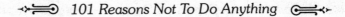

Hard work has never killed anyone,
but it frightens some people half to death.

Aldous Huxley

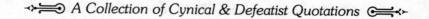

Marriage has many pains
but celibacy has no pleasures.

Samuel Johnson
Rasselas

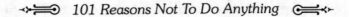

If it rained knowledge, I'd hold out my hand;
but I would not give myself the trouble
to go in quest of it.

Boswell
Life of Johnson

In this world nothing can be said to be certain,
except death and taxes.

Benjamin Franklin
letter to Jean-Baptiste Le Roy

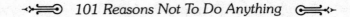

Cheer up, the worst is yet to come.

Philander Johnson
Shooting Stars

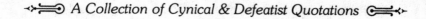

Thank heaven the sun has gone in,
and I don't have to go out and enjoy it.

Logan Pearsall Smith

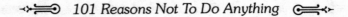

Call no man happy until he dies,
he is at best fortunate.

Plutarch
Solon

It is unfortunate, considering enthusiasm
moves the world, that so few enthusiasts
can be trusted to speak the truth.

A. J. Balfour

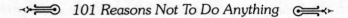

Marriage is a romance in which the
hero dies in the first chapter.

Anon
Quoted by Barbara Gourdy – Falling Angels

Like every man of sense and good feeling,
I abominate work.

Aldous Huxley

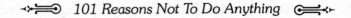

The lecture theatre – the place where information passes from the notebook of the lecturer to the notebook of the student without necessarily passing throught the mind of either.

Jim White

Mother is the dead heart of the family, spending father's earnings on consumer goods to enhance the environment in which he eats, sleeps and watches the television.

Germaine Greer
The Female Eunuch

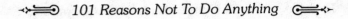

Brigands demand your money or your life;
women require both.

Samuel Butler

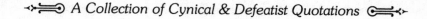

By working faithfully eight hours a day,
you may eventually get to be a boss
and work twelve hours a day.

Robert Frost

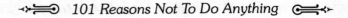

Life is too short to do anything for oneself
that one can pay others to do for one.

W. Somerset Maugham
The Summing Up

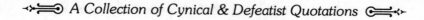

They say hard work never hurt anybody,
but I figure: why take the chance?

Ronald Reagan

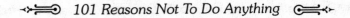

If I were a medical man, I should prescribe a
holiday to any patient who considered
his work important.

Bertrand Russell
Autobiography

I love mankind
– it's people I can't stand.

Charles M Schultz
Go Fly a Kite, Charlie Brown

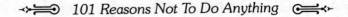

I never found the companion that was so
companionable as solitude.

Henry David Thoreau
Solitude

The majority of men devote the greater part
of their lives to making their remaining years unhappy.

Jean De La Bruyère

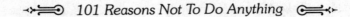

He that lives upon hope will die fasting.

Benjamin Franklin
Poor Richard's Almanac

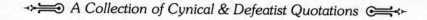

If people really liked to work,
we'd still be ploughing the land with
sticks and transporting goods on our backs.

William Feather

Time you can enjoy wasting
is never wasted time.

Anon

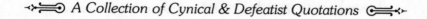

There are only three events in a man's life;
birth, life and death; he is not conscious of
being born, he dies in pain and he forgets to live.

Jean De La Bruyère

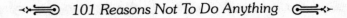
Ours is a world where people don't know
what they want and are willing to go
through hell to get it.

Don Marquis

Laziness implies a lot of intelligence. It is the normal healthy attitude of a man with nothing to do.

Sir Heneage Oglivie

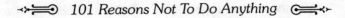

Anybody who works is a fool. I don't work,
I merely inflict myself on the public.

Robert Morley

Work is the only dirty four-letter
word in the language.

Abbie Hoffman
Harpers Magazine, 1970

You marry the man of your dreams, ladies,
but 14 years later you're married to a couch that burps.

Roseanne Barr
Roseanne, 1986

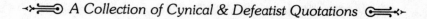

It's always been and always will be the
same in the world: the horse does the work
and the coachman is tipped.

Anon

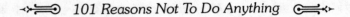

People would rather sleep their way through life
than stay awake for it.

Edward Albee

Life is a concentration camp.
You're stuck here and there's no way out
and you can only rage impotently
against your persecutors.

Woody Allen
Esquire, 1977

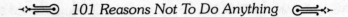

Life is a practical joke.

Paul Bocuse

Life is a shit sandwich and
everyday you take another bite.

Joe Schmidt

Life's a piece of shit,
when you look at it.

Eric Idle
Life Of Brian

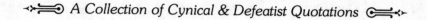

There is only the difference of a letter between the
beginning and the end of life - creation and cremation.

Sir Herbert Beerbohm Tree

Lord Illingworth:
The Book of Life begins with a man
and a woman in a garden.

Mrs Allonby:
It ends with Revelations.

Oscar Wilde
A Woman of No Importance

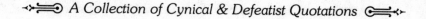

The shorter the hours, the larger the income. Don't get into the habit of putting in long hours or you may be set down into a permanent subordinate position.

George Ade
Fables

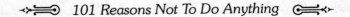

His sole concern with work was
considering how he might best avoid it.

Anatole France
Revolt of the Angels

Work is the scythe of time.

Napoleon Bonaparte, 1815

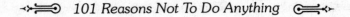

Set me anything to do as a task, and it is
inconceivable the desire I have to do something else.

George Bernard Shaw

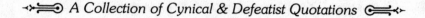

It is easier to admire hardwork if you don't do it.

Unknown
Meditations on Wall Street.

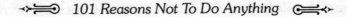

Work is the curse of the drinking classes.

Oscar Wilde

Life is a one way street.

Bernard Berenson
Notes, 1950

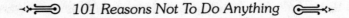

All of the animals excepting man know that
the principal business of life is to enjoy it.

Samuel Butler
Notebooks

Life ain't all beer and skittles, and more's the pity; but
what's the odds, so long as you're happy?

George du Maurier
Trilby

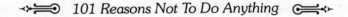

Life is like an onion: you peel off layer after layer and
then you find there is nothing in it.

James G Huneker

We are but tenants, and ... shortly the great Landlord will give us notice that our lease has expired.

Joseph Jefferson
Inscription on his monument

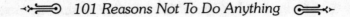

He beats the bush and another catches the bird.

Old French Proverb

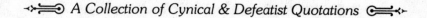

It is not necessary that a man should earn his living by the sweat of his brow, unless he sweats easier than I do.

Henry D Thoreau

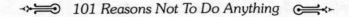

The brain is a wonderful organ.
It starts working the moment you get up,
and does not stop until you get into the office.

Attributed to Robert Frost

In a hierarchy every employee tends to rise
to his level of incompetence.

Laurence J. Peter
The Peter Principle

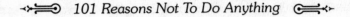

One should not exaggerate the importance of trifles.
Life, for instance, is much too short to be taken seriously.

Attributed to Nicolas Bentley

Living is a sickness from which sleep provides relief
every sixteen hours.   [...] The Remedy is Death.

Nicolas Chamfort

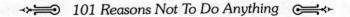

Thirty million, mostly fools.
[When asked the population of England]

Thomas Carlyle

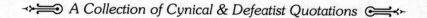

Life is just one damned thing after another.

Elbert Hubbard
A Thousand and One Epigrams

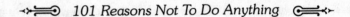

Life is as tedious as a twice-told tale
Vexing the dull ear of a drowsy man.

William Shakespeare
King John

It is better to be a fool than to be dead.

R L Stevenson

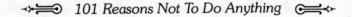

Friendship is a disinterested commerce between equals;
love an abject intercourse between tyrants and slaves.

Oliver Goldsmith

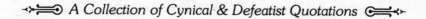

Work is accomplished by those employees who
have not yet reached their level of incompetence.

Laurence J Peter
The Peter Principle

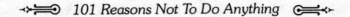

Life is a tragedy when seen in close-up,
but a comedy in long-shot.

Charlie Chaplin

Life is a jest; and all things show it.
I thought so once but now I know it.

John Gay
My Own Epitaph

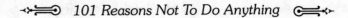

Life is one long process of getting tired.

Samuel Butler

Life would be tolerably agreeable if it
were not for its amusements.

Edward Bulwer-Lytton

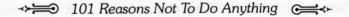

The basic fact about human existence
is not that it is a tragedy, but that it is a bore.

H. L. Mencken
Prejudices

I do not want people to be very agreeable, as it saves me
the trouble of liking them a great deal.

Jane Austen
Letters

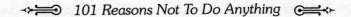

I have often thought upon death,
and I find it the least of all evils.

Francis Bacon
An Essay Upon Death

Never, ever, bloody anything ever.

Rick Mayall
Mr Jolly Lives Next Door

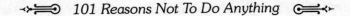

A person seldom falls sick, but the bystanders are animated with a faint hope that he will die.

Ralph Waldo Emerson

I hate quotations.

Ralph Waldo Emerson

If all the year were playing holidays,
To sport would be as tedious as to work;
But when they seldom come, they wish'd for come.

William Shakespeare
Henry IV

Who first invented Work–and tied the free
And holy-day rejoicing spirit down
To the ever-haunting importunity
Of business, in the green fields, and the town–
To plough–loom–anvil–spade–and, oh, most sad,
To this dry drudgery of desk's dead wood?

Charles Lamb
Letter to Barton

He may live without books, – what is knowledge but grieving?
He may live without hope, – what is hope but deceiving?
He may live without love, – what is passion but pining?
But where is the man that can live without dining?

Owen Meredith
Lucille

Man, I can assure you, is a nasty creature.

Molière

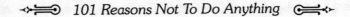

The ceaseless labour of your life is to
build the house of your death.

Montaigne

If one judges love by the majority of its effects, it is more
like hatred than like friendship.

Duc de la Rochefoucauld

If you give me six lines written by the most honest man, I will find something in them to hang him.

Attributed to Cardinal Richelieu

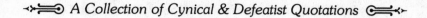

The world itself is but a large prison,
out of which some are daily led to execution.

Sir Walter Raleigh

'Blessed is the man who expects nothing, for he shall never be disappointed' was the ninth beatitude.

Alexander Pope
Letter to Fortescue

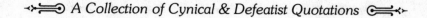

In the misfortunes of our best friends we
find something that is not unpleasing.

Duc De La Rochefoucauld

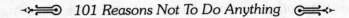

So little done, so much to do.

Cecil Rhodes
[Last words]